Exploring Caves

Written by Cassie Welsh

Celebration Press
Parsippany, New Jersey

Table of Contents

Inside a Cave

The inside of a cave is cool and dark. Sometimes rocks that look like icicles hang from the ceiling. They are called **stalactites**. Sometimes rocks that look like teeth rise up from the ground. They are called **stalagmites**. Both of these formations, as well as other cave formations, are **speleothems**.

Limestone Caves

This room is inside a **limestone cave**. It is bigger than 14 football fields and taller than a 25-story building! Limestone caves are the most common kind of cave. They are also the biggest.

How do limestone caves form? Rain picks up carbon dioxide from the air. It forms a solution that enters cracks in the earth. The solution eats away the limestone.

Rain

Carbon Dioxide

Limestone

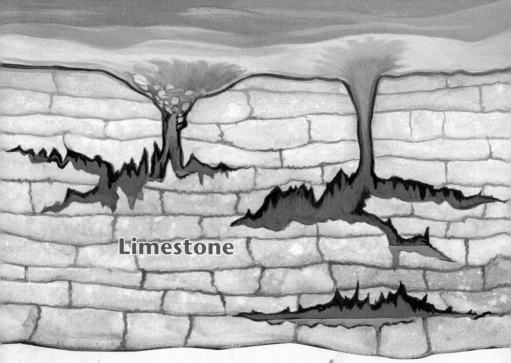

Limestone

Thousands of years pass. The holes get bigger and bigger until a cave forms.

Sometimes caves are made by underground rivers. At first the river cuts a path through the rock. Then the whole cave is filled with water. After many years the water drains out. Very large caves, or **caverns**, are often formed this way.

Sea Caves

Limestone caves aren't the only caves made by water. **Sea caves** are made when waves hit cliffs at the edge of the sea. These caves also take thousands of years to form.

Sea stars and crabs often live in pools of water in sea caves. Seals and sea lions may also make sea caves their home.

Lava Caves

Lava is melted rock. It is very, very hot. Lava is what comes out of a volcano. It can also flow like a river underneath layers of rock. Then it is called **magma**.

Lava caves form in lava that flows away from a volcano. Cold air hardens the lava into rock on the outside, but lava on the inside drains away. The hole left behind is like a tube. Lava caves usually have fewer rooms or branches than limestone caves.

Bat

Mouse

Blind Salamander

Cave Life

Lots of animals live in caves. Animals such as bats and mice sleep in caves. They go out at night to hunt. These animals live near the cave entrance.

Mushrooms

Blind Cave Fish

Other animals live deep inside caves. These animals are often blind. They don't need to see because it is always dark there.

Fungi, such as mushrooms, also grow in caves. Unlike green plants, fungi don't need any light to survive.

Spelunkers and Cave Dwellers

Today people who explore caves are called **spelunkers**. Thousands of years ago, however, people really lived in caves. We call them **cave dwellers**.

Spelunkers have found many pictures of animals and other things that cave dwellers painted on cave walls. They have also found tools that cave dwellers used.

Stone tools used by cave dwellers

Exploring and Visiting Caves

Exploring a cave is exciting, but it can also be dangerous. Spelunkers must be very careful to protect not only themselves but also the rocks and animals in the cave. They wear special helmets and use special tools so that they don't get hurt.

Glossary

cave dwellers people who lived in caves thousands of years ago

cavern a very large cave made by an underground river

fungi a group of living things, similar to plants, that do not need light to grow. Mushrooms are one example of fungi.

lava melted rock or magma that has burst from a volcano

lava cave a cave made by a river of lava

limestone cave a cave made by water cutting through limestone rock

magma melted rock beneath the earth's crust

sea cave a cave made by crashing waves wearing away the rocks of a sea cliff

speleothems minerals or formations added to a cave after it is created

spelunker a person who explores caves

stalactite a rock that hangs from the ceiling of a cave

stalagmite a rock that rises up from the ground of a cave